THE TORPEDO RUN

BY **LIN OLIVER**   ILLUSTRATED BY **CHARLES S. PYLE**

GREAT RAILWAY ADVENTURES
SERIES 1 • ADVENTURE 3
Learning Curve Publishing
Chicago

LIONEL
AMERICAN LEGEND

For Alan . . . my silent partner — L.O.

To Taylor, Craig, and Diana, the train crew who helped this consist to get out of the yard — C.P.

THE GREAT RAILWAY ADVENTURES BOOKS ARE IN MEMORY OF MURRAY SCHRAMM, GREAT FRIEND AND MENTOR.

Library of Congress Catalog Card Number: 98-85457

ISBN 1-890647-52-7 (hardbound)
ISBN 1-890647-55-1 (paperback)

10 9 8 7 6 5 4 3 2 1

Text set in 14 point Simoncini Garamond
Art direction and text design by Joy Chu

Printed in the United States of America

*T*HE TAXI BUMPED DOWN THE ROAD, COMING TO a stop in front of the huge train hangar. Maynard Henry had barely opened the door when Chief jumped out. The little dog chased his tail around and around, glad to be out of the car.

Tuck and Billie Holden stared out the window at the enormous building. With its lights glowing in the night sky, the hangar looked like a spaceship from a faraway planet.

Inside, train builders were working in secret to put the finishing touches on the *Torpedo*, the brand-new engine that no one had ever seen but everyone was calling the Locomotive of Tomorrow.

The door to the hangar swung open and Thaddeus Winterbottom stepped out. As president of the railroad, he was fond of giving long-winded speeches.

"Tonight," he began, clearing his throat mightily, "the *Torpedo* will set out on its first run. I'm proud to have the three of you join me on this historic occasion."

Billie, Tuck, and Mr. Henry started to go in the hangar, but Mr. Winterbottom pulled them back. He wasn't finished yet.

"We will travel in darkness," he went on, "making our grand entrance tomorrow morning at the World's Fair in New York. Mr. Henry, you have the honor of being the first engineer of the Locomotive of Tomorrow. Tuck and Billie, you will be its first passengers. Chief, you will be its first canine."

Chief wagged his tail happily, even though he had no idea what a canine was.

Inside the hangar, a giant blue locomotive was being lowered by a heavy crane.

"I give you the *Torpedo*." Mr. Winterbottom beamed. "The largest and fastest passenger engine ever built. You're looking at one million pounds of rolling steel."

Tuck and Billie stared in amazement. The *Torpedo* looked like a rocket. It was huge —
longer than fifteen automobiles lined up end to end. Mr. Henry gazed up at the beautiful
engine.

"Well, I'll be," he said simply. "Well, I'll be."

As Tuck watched the workers set the *Torpedo* on the tracks, he felt like the luckiest boy
in the world. He couldn't believe it was only a few weeks ago that he had dreamed of a
glass train car with high domed windows all around. His mother and father had designed a
model of Tuck's Dome Car and entered it in the Invention of Tomorrow contest at the
World's Fair.

When Tuck and Billie decided to surprise their parents at the World's Fair, they never
imagined that they would be lucky enough to arrive in New York on the first run of the
Torpedo. Mr. Winterbottom invited them on board as a reward for rescuing Maynard
Henry's train, the *President Washington*, from a dangerous crash.

Now, here they were, about to take part in a historic occasion.

It was late at night when the *Torpedo* was finally ready to go. Mr. Winterbottom stepped forward and cleared his throat. The workers knew what that meant. He was going to make a speech. They scattered quickly.

Noticing that he had no audience, Mr. Winterbottom decided to cut short his remarks.

Mr. Henry climbed into the *Torpedo*'s cab. Tuck and Billie were already inside. They had never seen so many dials and switches and levers. "What are all these things for?" asked Billie. She reached for a shiny black knob.

"Don't touch that," Mr. Henry cried. "It's the steam release!"

It was too late. Billie had already turned the knob.

A blast of steam shot from the engine, and a cloud filled the platform, covering Mr. Winterbottom from head to toe. Although he had disappeared from view entirely, he could be heard sputtering inside the thick white cloud.

"Mr. Winterbottom," yelled Tuck. "Are you all right?"

"Not to worry, young man," Mr. Winterbottom answered from inside the haze. "Historic occasions often have rocky beginnings."

Mr. Winterbottom retired to the parlor car to change his suit and rest up. The others waited on the tracks for the all-clear signal. At last it came.

"Well, whippersnappers," Mr. Henry said. "Looks like we're ready to roll."

He took a deep breath and fired up the mighty engine. Billie could see that his hand was shaking as he took hold of the throttle. She placed her small hand over his.

"Don't worry, Mr. Henry," she said. "You're going to do great."

Billie kept her hand on his as the *Torpedo* pulled out of the hangar into the dark night.

They rolled smoothly along the tracks, passing sleeping villages and shadowy towns. Only a full moon and the engine's bright headlight lit the way. The measured beats of the wheels pounded out a steady rhythm. *Clickity-clack. Clickity-clack.*

"Let's see what she's really got," Mr. Henry said.

He opened up the throttle, letting more and more steam do more and more work. When the *Torpedo* reached one hundred miles per hour, Tuck and Billie hooted and hollered. They felt like they were flying.

As the night passed, Tuck and Billie grew tired.

"Why don't you catch a little shut-eye," suggested Mr. Henry.

"I can't sleep," said Billie. "I miss my parents."

Tuck put his arm around Billie. "Remember what Mom and Dad told us," he said gently. "No matter how far away they are, they're always just on the other side of the train whistle."

Mr. Henry pointed to the cord above his head.

"Go ahead and blow that thing," he said. "Say good night to your folks."

Billie pulled on the cord. The whistle sounded. It was the same sound their family heard every day back home in California when the *Daylight Limited* passed their house. Billie smiled. The whistle reminded her of her parents. She knew that somewhere out there, they were thinking of her, too. She snuggled up next to Tuck, and soon they were both asleep.

Tuck and Billie woke up at dawn.

"We're not far from New York now," Mr. Henry told them.

Tuck squinted out the window. In the morning light, he could see a bridge up ahead. Suddenly, two men appeared in the middle of the tracks.

"Watch out!" Tuck cried. "There are people on the bridge!"

Mr. Henry grabbed for the brake. As the train slowed, they saw the men more clearly. One was thin and wore a straw hat. The other was tall with bulging muscles everywhere.

The *Torpedo* ground to a stop just before the bridge.

Mr. Henry jumped out of the engine, followed by Tuck and Billie. His eyes flashed in anger.

"What in tarnation do you think you're doing on these tracks?" he demanded.

The door of the parlor car flew open, and Mr. Winterbottom stepped out. He had been sleeping, and his night mask still covered one eye.

"Nice mask, Pops," said the man in the straw hat, "but Halloween is over."

"You are speaking to Thaddeus Winterbottom, sir, and I don't like your tone of voice," said Mr. Winterbottom. "I assume you are the person responsible for this sudden stop."

"Allow me to introduce myself," said the man. "Scoop Jackson, photographer extraordinaire." He pointed to the tall man with the bulging arms. "This is my associate, Tiny."

Tiny grinned and flexed his muscles. Chief growled at him.

Scoop crossed the bridge and approached the train. He pulled a camera out of his bag. "I just want a couple of pictures of the *Torpedo*," he said. "I'm going to sell them to the newspapers before anyone else can."

"You'll do no such thing," said Mr. Winterbottom. "Hundreds of photographers are waiting to take our picture at the World's Fair."

"That's why they call me Scoop." Scoop grinned. "I always get there first. The papers pay a pretty penny for that."

"This is an outrage!" roared Mr. Winterbottom. "We're leaving!"

"Not so fast, Summerbottom," Scoop said. "You're going to wait right here until I deliver the pictures to the paper. Tiny will make sure you don't leave."

Tiny picked up an iron bar and bent it as if it were rubber. He wasn't about to let them leave.

Scoop began shooting pictures of the *Torpedo*. Mr. Winterbottom was fuming.

"The mayor of New York is due to meet us at nine o'clock," he told Scoop angrily. "They've scheduled a ticker-tape parade."

"Too bad you won't be there to see it." Scoop smiled.

"We're going to miss the contest, too," Billie said to Tuck. There was sadness in her voice.

Tuck was not about to let anyone make them miss the Invention of Tomorrow contest. He and Billie had traveled too far to give up now. He glanced around, searching for an idea. Then, he remembered — the shiny black knob inside the cab.

Tuck turned to Scoop.

"Excuse me, Mr. Jackson," he said, "but you'd get a better picture if you stood over here next to the wheels."

"Good idea, kid," said Scoop. "You've got a real eye."

Scoop moved closer to the train. He was so busy shooting his pictures that he didn't see Tuck jump into the cab and turn the shiny black knob.

A blast of steam shot out from under the wheels, covering Scoop from head to toe. He disappeared from view, but he could be heard sputtering inside the thick white cloud.

"Tiny!" he yelled. "I can't see. Do something!"

Tiny flexed his muscles. Quick thinking was not his specialty.

As Scoop tried to find his way out of the cloud, everyone jumped back on the *Torpedo* — everyone, that is, but Chief. The little dog growled at Tiny, then lunged at his pants leg, tugging and snarling.

"Chief," yelled Billie, as Mr. Henry fired up the engine. "Come on!"

Chief gave Tiny's pants one last tug. Down they came! Chief jumped on board and the engine pulled out. Tiny tried to run after it, but he tripped and landed on Scoop. The two men toppled over and fell splashing into the river.

Mr. Henry opened up the throttle and went full steam ahead. The *Torpedo* shot down the tracks like a cannonball.

Everyone inside laughed and cheered.

"New York City, here we come!" shouted Tuck.

"Indeed!" Mr. Winterbottom laughed, slapping Tuck on the back. "Indeed!"

Throngs of people surrounded the *Torpedo* as it pulled into the New York World's Fair. The mayor was there and reporters from all over the world. Cameras flashed and bands played. It was a glorious moment.

Tuck and Billie searched the crowd for their mother and father. Tuck wondered if they would ever find their parents in this sea of faces. It seemed impossible.

Then he had an idea.

"Mr. Henry," he yelled into the cab. "Would you please sound the whistle? Give it four short blasts."

Four short blasts — the signal for the Holdens to stop what they were doing and run to the tracks to watch the train thunder by.

Inside the exhibition hall, the Invention of Tomorrow contest was in full swing. Mr. and Mrs. Holden were standing by their model of the Dome Car when they heard the *Torpedo's* whistle.

"Did you hear that?" Mr. Holden said to his wife.

Mr. and Mrs. Holden both knew that the judges would be at their booth any minute, but they didn't care. They grabbed their hats and followed the familiar sound. Somewhere in their hearts, for a reason neither of them understood, they felt that something wonderful was waiting for them on that train . . . just on the other side of the whistle.

Mr. and Mrs. Holden ran to the platform and pressed their way into the crowd that had gathered in front of the *Torpedo*. Tuck and Billie saw them immediately.

"Mom! Dad!" they yelled. "We're here! We're here!"

Tuck and Billie jumped off the train and ran into their parents' arms.

"This is a miracle," said Mr. Holden, kissing his children's smiling faces.

"How on earth did you get here?" asked Mrs. Holden. She was overcome with joy.

Tuck and Billie laughed and hugged their parents hard. There would be time to tell their story later. For now, just being together was enough.

The Dome Car didn't win the Invention of Tomorrow contest. A strange little box that brought talking pictures into people's living rooms did. It was called the television.

The Dome Car did win a special blue ribbon, though. Even better, Mr. Winterbottom saw it and decided to introduce the first Dome Car on his railroad.

"Mr. Holden," he said, "you will be the chief builder. Mrs. Holden, you will be the chief designer. Tuck and Billie, you will be the chief dreamers."

Chief jumped into Mr. Winterbottom's arms and licked him on his bushy whiskers.

"And you"— Mr. Winterbottom laughed —"will be the chief Chief."

Five years later, the Holdens, accompanied by Mr. Henry and Mr. Winterbottom, rode their Dome Car on its first cross-country trip. Thousands of passengers would follow them, enjoying the beauty of the moving landscape through windows that arched up to the sky.

From their train car made of glass, Tuck and Billie Holden looked out at sparkling rivers and green forests, fields of wheat, and snowy mountains. They smiled proudly. In that moment, they knew that dreams really can come true.

THE TORPEDO RUN

IF YOU RODE THE TRAIN . . .

If you were traveling overland in 1939 when *The Torpedo Run* takes place, chances are, you would have taken a train. There were no passenger jet planes back then. Train travel was an exciting adventure. It gave passengers the chance to see all the beautiful landscape of the country. It was a time when everyone wasn't in such a hurry to get somewhere.

- If you lived in a big city, there was usually a huge train station with a large waiting room, high ceilings, and trains coming and going all day.

- Your train would have been streamlined, painted in bright colors, and pulled by a sleek locomotive. Your train might have been pulled by the *Torpedo*, the largest, heaviest, and fastest engine in the world. It was 140 feet long, weighed one million pounds, and could go faster than 100 miles per hour.

- If you were traveling overnight, you might have slept in your seat all night. If you had a lot of money, you could choose a sleeping compartment, complete with a private toilet and sink. Many trains had showers, a barber, a nurse, and even a secretary for those who had to work.

- If you went exploring, you might have wandered into the mail car. Postal workers spent the entire trip sorting the mail that they picked up and dropped off at each train station or town.

• At mealtime, you would have eaten in the dining car. Dining cars were like fancy restaurants with linen tablecloths, china plates, and fresh cut flowers on every table. The food was delicious. You could get a complete dinner, including dessert, for $1.35.

• After dinner, you might have gone to the observation car, the last car on the train, where you could talk, read, and look out the large windows at the passing scenery. There was even a speedometer to tell you how fast the train was going.

IF YOU WANT TO LEARN MORE ABOUT TRAINS, ASK YOUR LIBRARIAN FOR SUGGESTIONS. THERE ARE MANY WONDERFUL BOOKS ON TRAIN TRAVEL, THE HISTORY OF TRAINS, AND MODEL TRAINS.

The Torpedo was called the Locomotive of Tomorrow when it was first displayed at the 1939 New York World's Fair. Its engine weighed more than one million pounds.